Our American Flag

by Mary Firestone

illustrated by Matthew Skeens

PICTURE WINDOW BOOKS
Minneapolis, Minnesota

Special thanks to our advisers for their expertise:

Kevin Byrne, Ph.D., Professor of History
Gustavus Adolphus College

Susan Kesselring, M.A., Literacy Educator
Rosemount–Apple Valley–Eagan (Minnesota) School District

Editor: Jill Kalz
Designer: Nathan Gassman
Page Production: Tracy Kaehler and Ellen Schofield
Creative Director: Keith Griffin
Editorial Director: Carol Jones
The illustrations in this book were created digitally.
Photo credit: Shutterstock/J. Helgason, 23

Picture Window Books
1710 Roe Crest Drive
North Mankato, MN 56003
www.capstonepub.com

All books published by Picture Window Books
are manufactured with paper containing at least
10 percent post-consumer waste.

Library of Congress Cataloging-in-Publication Data
Firestone, Mary.
Our American flag / by Mary Firestone ; illustrated by Matthew Skeens.
p. cm. — (American symbols)
Includes bibliographical references and index.
ISBN: 978-1-4048-2212-2 (library binding)
ISBN: 978-1-4048-2218-4 (paperback)
1. Flags—United States—History—Juvenile literature. I. Skeens, Matthew.
II. Title. III. American symbols (Picture Window Books)
CR113.F465 2007
929.9'20973—dc22   2006003375

Printed in the United States of America in North Mankato, Minnesota.
062012   006741R

Table of Contents

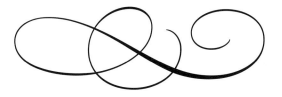

I'm Mary Pickersgill.
I sewed one of the most famous flags in the history of the United States. The country's national anthem was written about it! The U.S. flag has gone through many changes over the years. Here is its story.

Why Do Countries Have Flags?

Countries around the world use flags as symbols. The U.S. flag is a symbol of freedom and patriotism. It is also a symbol of the country's land and people.

During the Revolutionary War (1775–1783), soldiers from the American colonies carried all kinds of flags into battle. They didn't have one official flag. Because of that, soldiers often didn't know who was a friend and who was an enemy.

Flags of the American colonies had pictures of snakes, crosses, and pine trees on them.

One Common Flag

In 1775, Benjamin Franklin suggested that the American colonies use one common flag. Soon they all agreed to fly the Grand Union flag. This flag had 13 red and white stripes. Each stripe stood for one of the 13 colonies. The flag also had a small British Union flag in the canton. A canton is the upper-left section of a flag.

The original 13 colonies were Virginia, Massachusetts, New Hampshire, Maryland, Connecticut, Rhode Island, Delaware, North Carolina, South Carolina, New Jersey, New York, Pennsylvania, and Georgia.

The First Official Flag

In 1777, Congress wanted the flag to look more American. They removed the British Union flag from the canton and put 13 stars in its place. Like the stripes, each star stood for one of the 13 colonies.

This flag became the official flag of the United States on June 14, 1777. But people wondered: How many points should the stars have? Should they be put in a circle or in rows? The country had all kinds of different flags again!

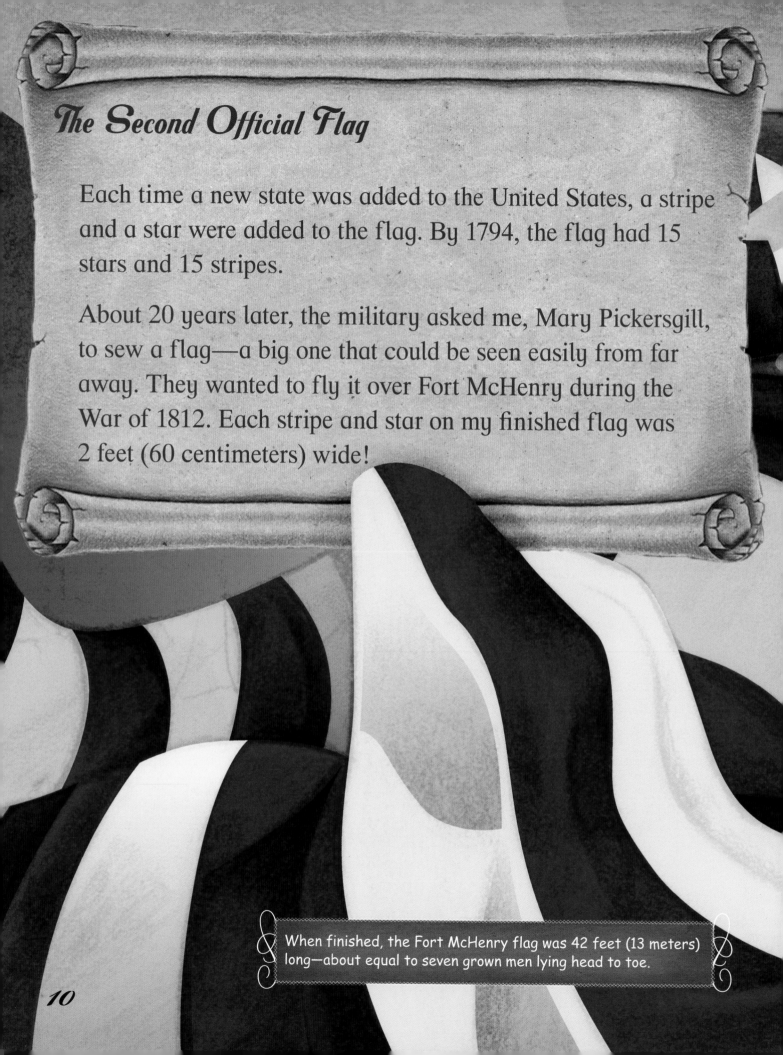

The Second Official Flag

Each time a new state was added to the United States, a stripe and a star were added to the flag. By 1794, the flag had 15 stars and 15 stripes.

About 20 years later, the military asked me, Mary Pickersgill, to sew a flag—a big one that could be seen easily from far away. They wanted to fly it over Fort McHenry during the War of 1812. Each stripe and star on my finished flag was 2 feet (60 centimeters) wide!

When finished, the Fort McHenry flag was 42 feet (13 meters) long—about equal to seven grown men lying head to toe.

The Star-Spangled Banner

The British bombed Fort McHenry for 25 hours. When the smoke cleared, my beautiful flag was still flying.

A lawyer named Francis Scott Key saw the flag and wrote a poem about it. The poem was later set to music, and the song became the national anthem of the United States.

The Star-Spangled Banner

(first of four verses)   words by Francis Scott Key

O say, can you see, by the dawn's early light,

What so proudly we hailed at the twilight's last gleaming?

Whose broad stripes and bright stars, through the perilous fight,

O'er the ramparts we watched, were so gallantly streaming?

And the rocket's red glare, the bombs bursting in air,

Gave proof through the night that our flag was still there.

O say does that star-spangled banner yet wave

O'er the land of the free, and the home of the brave?

Back to 13 Stripes

In 1818, five new states joined the country. Congress members knew that if they kept adding stripes and stars for each new state, the flag would grow too big. So, they went back to 13 stripes, which stood for the original 13 colonies. Only a star would be added for each new state. But people still lined up the stars in different ways.

In 1818, the U.S. flag had 20 stars, which stood for the country's 20 states.

The Flag Grows

In 1912, President William Howard Taft put the flag's stars in official order. The country then had 48 states, so the flag had six rows of stars, with eight stars in each row. Each star had one point facing up.

More changes to the flag came in 1959 and 1960.
Two stars were added as Alaska and Hawaii became states.

Today, the U.S. flag has 50 stars for 50 states.

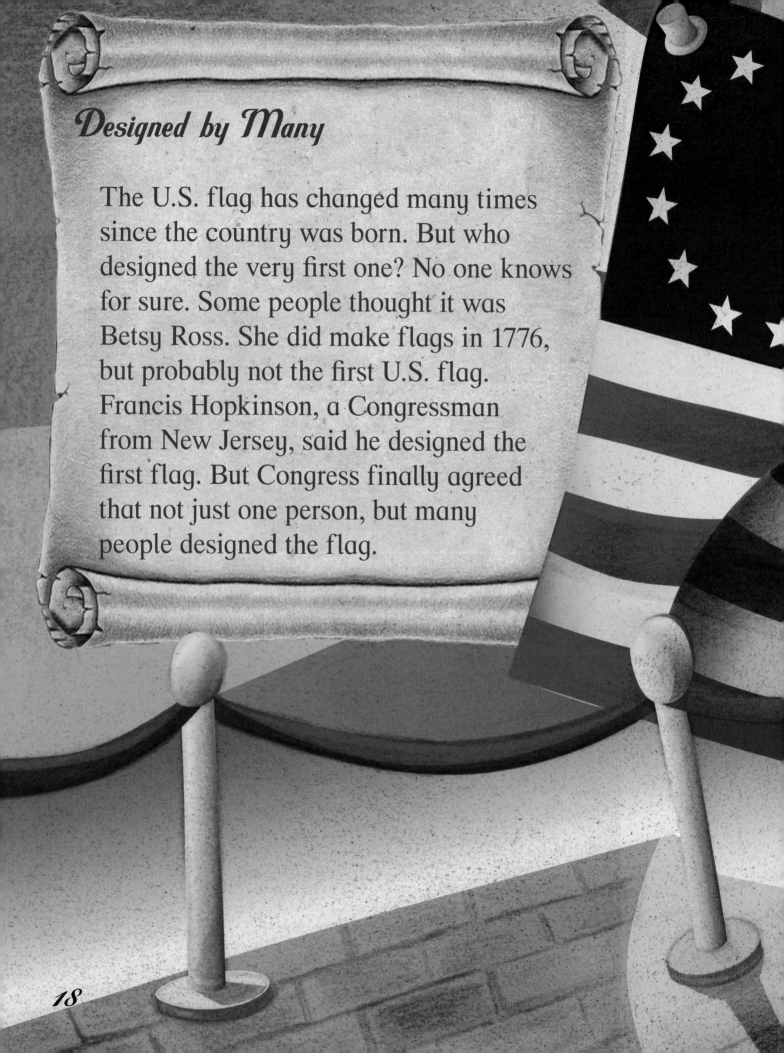

Designed by Many

The U.S. flag has changed many times since the country was born. But who designed the very first one? No one knows for sure. Some people thought it was Betsy Ross. She did make flags in 1776, but probably not the first U.S. flag. Francis Hopkinson, a Congressman from New Jersey, said he designed the first flag. But Congress finally agreed that not just one person, but many people designed the flag.

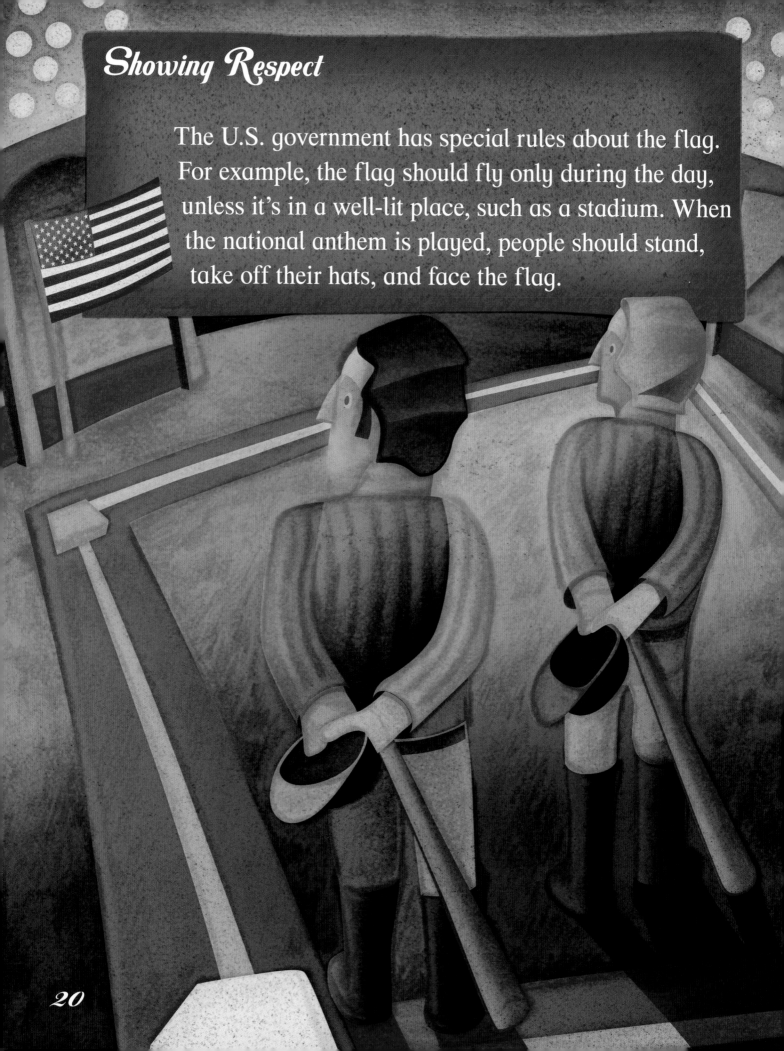

Showing Respect

The U.S. government has special rules about the flag. For example, the flag should fly only during the day, unless it's in a well-lit place, such as a stadium. When the national anthem is played, people should stand, take off their hats, and face the flag.

The flag should not touch the ground. It should not fly
in bad weather, either. All of these rules are part of the
U.S. Flag Code.

I hope you've enjoyed learning about the U.S. flag. For more than 200 years, it has been a symbol of Americans' freedom and patriotism. Fly it proudly!

Flag Facts

❧ The U.S. flag has many nicknames. Some people call it the Stars and Stripes. Others call it the Star-Spangled Banner, Old Glory, and the Red, White, and Blue.

❧ Today, the Fort McHenry flag rests in the Smithsonian Institution, in Washington, D.C. A curtain protects it from light and dust. Visitors can view the flag for only a few moments once every hour, when the curtain is pulled back.

❧ On August 3, 1949, President Harry S. Truman made June 14 National Flag Day.

❧ Vexillology (vek-seh-LAH-leh-jee) is the study of flags. Someone who knows a lot about flags is called a vexillologist (vek-seh-LAH-leh-jist).

The U.S. Flag

Glossary

Benjamin Franklin — an American inventor, author, and Founding Father (a signer of the Constitution)

colonies — lands away from home that are controlled by the homeland, such as the American colonies of Great Britain

Congress — the group of people in the U.S. government who make laws

Fort McHenry — a fort in Baltimore, Maryland, that successfully defended Baltimore Harbor from the British navy in the War of 1812

national anthem — a country's special patriotic song

official — approved by the government

patriotism — love for one's own country

Revolutionary War — (1775–1783) the Colonies' fight for freedom from Great Britain; the Colonies later became the United States of America

symbols — objects that stand for something else

War of 1812 — (1812–1815) a war between the United States and Great Britain over unfair British control of shipping; often called the "Second War of Independence"

To Learn More

At the Library

Douglas, Lloyd G. *The American Flag.* New York: Children's Press, 2003.

Gray, Susan H. *The American Flag.* Minneapolis: Compass Point Books, 2002.

Martin, Bill, Jr. *I Pledge Allegiance.* Cambridge, Mass.: Candlewick Press, 2002.

Thomson, Sara L. *Stars and Stripes.* New York: HarperCollins Publishers, 2003.

On the Web

FactHound offers a safe, fun way to find Web sites related to topics in this book. All of the sites on FactHound have been researched by our staff.

1. Visit *www.facthound.com*
2. Type in this special code: 1404822127
3. Click on the FETCH IT button.

Your trusty FactHound will fetch the best sites for you!

24

Index

Look for all of the books in the American Symbols series:

The Great Seal of the United States
   1-4048-2214-3
Our American Flag
   1-4048-2212-7
Our National Anthem
   1-4048-2215-1
The Statue of Liberty
   1-4048-2216-X
The U.S. Constitution
   1-4048-2643-2
The White House
   1-4048-2217-8